The Yellow House

ROBIN BEHN

SPUYTEN DUYVIL

New York City

Acknowledgments

Poems from *The Yellow House* have appeared in the following journals, to whose editors grateful acknowledgment is made: *The Alembic*: "Reading in the Yellow House." *Born Magazine*: "Below the Cellar of the Yellow House There is Another Set of Stairs." *Caffeine Destiny*: "Yellow House Isogloss," "Lyric Interlude." *Crazyhorse*: "Aspirations of the Yellow House." *Columbia: A Journal of Arts and Letters*: "Waves." *Cue: A Journal of Prose Poetry*: "The Boy Asks," "Old Distance Woman Has Asked the Yellow House for a Book," "Where the Horse Went." *Field*: "The Yellow House Gives Tour Number One of the Big Art Book," "Tour Number Two: Unveiling," "Horse Between Tours," "Tour Number Three." *The Journal*: "The Yellow House Writes a Story for the Boy," "Red and Black Days." *The Iowa Review*: "Thought is Allowed." *The Manhattan Review*: "Chandelier," "A Pattern Language," "Above the Attic of the Yellow House There is Another Set of Stairs," "Distances of the Yellow House." *Mid-American Review*: "The Other." *New Orleans Review*: "Anthelion." *Perihelion*: "Hydrangea." *Ploughshares*: "Origin, Dark Yellow." *PMS poemmemoirstory*, "Yellow Morning," "The Floating Room." *poetrymagazine.com*: "In Dreams She is Permitted to Return to the Yellow Room." *Spoon River Poetry Review*: "Glove." *TriQuarterly*: "The Yellow House Alone in Snow," "Pursuit of the Yellow House." *Volt*: "Yellow Doors." "Pursuit of the Yellow House" also appeared in *Pushcart Prize XXX*. "Anthelion," "Red and Black Days," and "Waves" also appeared on *Verse Daily*. Some of these poems were featured on *poetrymagazine.com*. A number of these poems were included in *American Alphabets: 25 Contemporary Poets*, ed. David Walker, Oberlin College Press, 2006.

Abiding thanks to Chard, Bruce, Clare, Chris, Mirjana, Melissa and, in memory, Rane and Deborah; and to Waxwing Band, The Ragdale Foundation, The Corporation of Yaddo, and University of Alabama and Vermont College of Fine Arts students and colleagues for friendship, time, space, art, poems, and music. Paintings by Mirjana Ugrinov, Melissa Herrington, Wassily Kandinsky, and Paul Klee have been crucial and delightful.

Library of Congress Cataloging-in-Publication Data

Behn, Robin.
The yellow house / Robin Behn.
p. cm.
ISBN 978-1-933132-76-1
I. Title.
PS3552.E412Y45 2010
811'.54--dc22

2011009936

The Yellow House

Contents

III.

Color cannot stand alone; it cannot dispense with
boundaries of some kind.   WASSILY KANDINSKY

This house was drawn for them
it looks like a real house
perhaps they will move in today
into ephemeral dusk and
move out of that into night
selective night with trees,

The darkened copies of all trees.
BARBARA GUEST

In Order of Appearance

the horse

the boy

the house

the woman

the Other

the man

old distance man

old distance woman

the prophet

dear one

I.

THE YELLOW HOUSE WRITES A STORY FOR THE BOY

Once upon time, a horse and its rider came to a place where squares of light shone out from a room of air, out and out into the snow. *Golden paddock* is what the horse was thinking. *Halfway up this steep hill is plenty*, thought the boy. The doorway where snow wasn't was as wide and as tall and as still as a horse when it is sleeping in its stall, and so the horse went in and the boy on its back went in, too.

Inside was a cube in the shape of a bale of hay, and another cube that was a little table, and upon it a curve which was a spoon for hot chocolate which was waiting for the boy, he could smell it.

What?

O.K., and another hot chocolate for the horse.

The earth turned a little and the moon rose a little until the shadow of the horse lying down, hooves tucked up under, exactly matched the shadow of the room of air. The way a valentine takes on the shape of swelling and the shape of cutting and sweet thinking.

The boy lay down very close to the horse. Then the letter *r* lay down on its side, very close to the boy. And when he awoke, the boy was in a house and the horse was still huddled inside the yellow glow. And the house said, *Oh, O.K., you can ride your horse inside.*

YELLOW DOORS

Guillotine between
want and what's
served up.

Hardback, half.
Breastplate of storm.
Shut nerve chute.

Dizzyness, creased.
Turn-end, near-end, end-run, shackle.
Part and parting. Hair. Their.

A roaring, revolving.
A strickling of shores.
The dead-as-a reprise.

Keypads: gems, gum.
Heart-jamb, am-jamb.
Syzygy struck dumb.

A dromedary stillness
and the deckled edge,
flung.

One rub. Two views.
Stoop, and strip.
Hob, nail, polish, polish, lash, polish, gape.

Hinge twinge just
as the ribs swing wide
with a knock.

Aboard.
Abroad.
Inside.

ORIGIN, DARK YELLOW

Slice of yellow wind in yellow curtains
she sewed though that first house was never hers
except where the rod went through.
Breeze does it.
                    Or snow on pines. Faint clink
of yellowing spoons. Or crow-call piercing snow-pine
reflected in the spoon-shaped past,
its wing its crescent moon. Seeking any equally
black thing.
                    There, in those high rooms.
The landlord's piano and arpeggios of dust.
The angles of three rooms and the constant
vectoring. Every tangent outward
boomeranged back in.
                    But the man from Africa
coming up the stairs. Admiring, imagine,
the curtains. Coming up. Which made for stairs
which made for going down. To the world.
Him teaching her to loosen earth the
Zimbabwe way, small patches of stubbornness
and the single hoe.
                    What does the Other do?
She must have known at one point how to wait
upon the ground, smiling and watching.
She must have known the swing as of an ax
and then the boot, and then the bearing down.
The seeds and finally blossoming. The bearing
baring.
        This squash.
                    It is the color of
those strands of golden fur caught
in the grain of wood—his cat liked

the top drawer, soft among her softest things.
What they left there has been allowed
its daily audience with light
                              as long
as someone else lives there.
Dressing in the mornings.
Opening and closing things.
His dark yell, her yellow tears,
these twenty years.

ASPIRATIONS OF THE YELLOW HOUSE

Sometimes the yellow house wants
a public assignment

curved brow of school bus
crossing guard sash swatch

cheery cloth to sop
spittle from the oldest lips

library velo-card
pet shop's pet

iguana's awesome
dewlap

but seeing as how the yellow
jobs are already taken

uselessness becomes its motto
privacy its anthem

yellow tooth in a row of
better teeth it stands

through winter the snow going
yellow at its feet and sinking

into the muddy muck and mouth
of every living thing

then all around it troops of daffodils
blow their fancy horns and take a bow—

no one in the yellow house
knows its thwarted dreams

although the stairs do creak sometimes
as if a thing has turned around

to climb back to the stars,
and the windows, in the evening, have an aspect,

a dark, expectant, broken, floating, useless
telescope aspect,

but that goes away
when they are lit from within.

THE OTHER

It started and it starts
in the throat, then and now,

something in the lungs
passing through the rustle

and tremor through the
tear and tear because

the wind the voice is
stirs up bloody leaves

that make the body red inside
when read inside by light or a hand

It started when she heard him speak
it started when she heard him speak

it didn't, by then, matter what
he said he played the language like an

instrument, the pressure, imagine,
temples beading outward on the

crumhorn player's brow how
shining-wet and how the tiny un-im-

portant un-improveable in-
extractable song shuttling there among

locked woes is really less
than atoms than

electrons crazy inside atoms in
the small wood barrel where

the reed is mounted like a tongue
that has nowhere to strike but back at song

(the prisoner's dinner passed, now,
through the metal smile and the smell

of what might have been
withdrawing as the plate is withdrawn)--

His voice made her think like that.
His voice made her, think, like *that*.

CHANDELIER

Didn't we notice light's yellowing trapeze?
The drifting man-of-war? The cake frosted with shards?
Spider tabernacle brooding over the uncleared table?
That they could have swooned beneath
in some old age?
How old *is* the house?
How old the maker's mind when the thing it makes is older?
Light pricking itself, nervously, on dust.
Prom dress never taken from the hanger
that time shredded into a huge screaming corsage.
Shall we invite it to dance?
Shimmy those facets and aspects?
Vibrate like a hive from which drip
fears' tiers and tears?
When they bought the house
wasn't there the option to buy it without it?
How much for the brilliant bend
of neck like a tortured swan's,
the ladder fluttering below?
Do they still make these bulbs
like the torturer's tongue on fire?
Where are the gloves calibrated
for the caressing of dust?
And now what should they do with them?
Wash the dirt off light? In with their shirts?
The house-heart with their hearts?
Who just stormed out into the murderous glint
and who screamed like bloody murder
take your goddamn gloves and who
kept the shatter wired like a jaw together, after?

Reading in the Yellow House

Sometimes for two weeks at a time
she and the boy would be alone
with the yellow and the house.

And by the seventh day
they would turn, both of them,
the color of privacy, and stay that way,

even or especially
when they walked down the hill
together as if under one yellow umbrella

to go to the public library
whose yellowing volumes had once, in an hour,
by the frantic and heroic and thoroughly acclaimed

actions of five passing adolescents,
been rescued by a kind of book-brigade
from the flash flood.

Did we know about the yellow river, its fevers?
Did we know about the noble youth
the boy might, here, become?

The yellow house, above it all, would wait
for their return with the five unread volumes
and give them the yellow chair to read in,

and listen hard, itself, because stories never last
half as long as they should.
This is how the yellow house came to decide

it would be a place they could actually live in
and let their stories story it
so they would never die.

Distances of the Yellow House

Here in the turning
    of world and woe,
far from the yellow house,
    old distance man lies luring

death with a pole
    and a line so long
the years slip off
    the hook of his right, dead hand.

How can the house
    which feels, innermost,
the groan of its tree-wide beams
    surrendering,

micron by lichen,
    sag by seize by sigh by sooth
to impatient Earth,
    talk,

since he can't,
    to—which god?
of time? of thine?
    of tenant and argument?

hatch and dispatch?
    of ooze?
of brains
    in never-ending rain?

And so it goes on,
    the old man in his bed,
more than half dead,
    the house on its distant hill.

Yellow of jaundice,
    of poultice.
Of wings, of shine and shrine.
    Of watchface

he wore through a war.
    Of shredding paint and skin.
It would take just one
    to invite the other in.

THE FLOATING ROOM

What thing keeps them,
the woman and the Other,
time's conscripts, in this room
floating above time?

Her entire body bent
in the shape of a hook or a swan.
His entire body bent
in the shape of a hook or a swan.

Perhaps a half-swan each.
Yes. One whole swan, one seeking.
Which is why the tying and untying
of the water's silken knot.

There is some language in the background
where someone is assessing something
created by someone who seems to know
about the inner life of things.

But there are no things here.
No silk, hook, hat, knot, swan.
No one else in any sort of world will ever know this
swanning and unswanning.

ANTHELION

When there was nothing left to rearrange—
not hours, not food, not bed; not filigree
of the sound words made still hovering, estranged
from he or she who finally had agreed
the air, the many airs, they breathed and were
were dead—and they became their shoes,
staring down in the other's sight like something cowering
from moonlight, the moon as big as a town
lowered upon a town, eye upon closed eye,
heart wrapped in its own singed shadow pressed
upon its other shadow, still, they kept
on pacing: omen and phenomenon, falconer and –ress,
until the bird, if it was a bird, went blind
inside the hood. The yellow fire was its mind.

YELLOW MORNING

She awoke deep into the morning,
    forgiving words.

Forgiving how they want to make
    the whole world one color.

Forgiving how that color is loneliness incarnate.
    Forgiving how they persist,

building themselves an altar
    peopled with people, thinged with things,

and touched, sun or no sun, with sun:
    she awoke so deep into the morning

time had gone pungent and dim
    like the smell of an old locked trunk

stirred by a slow ray of light,
    within.

This is the dream of the woman,
    and this is the dream about the woman

another woman, her/not-her,
    woke in the middle of, and wept.

Outside, a fledgling
    —filthy lump upon a wet, black bough—

punctured daylight with its high cry,
    the sound of it shredding time

—*a nest, a nest, a nest*—
    until an adult the color of blood

appeared and put his blunt beak down
        into the tiny throat.

But then it woke again,
        not trusting the dream of trust,

and cried, and cried-and-cried
        —*for-SA-ken, for-SA-ken*—

so that an adult the color of blood rolled in the earth
        appeared and put her whole blunt beak

down into the throat and held it there
        the length of time it takes

in love, for the grail to be passed,
        and then, and then, it could sleep.

Who fed the birds?
        It happened outside of words.

Black Oil Sunflower Seed?
        Whatever. A need.

The Yellow House Combs the Stacks Near the Big Art Books

Little black smell, little black smell.
Rowing, rowing.
Little black smell, little black smell.
Rowing, rowing.

Skyline under a ledge. Skyline under a ledge.
Skinny tall house, skinny tall house,
brown tan black blue green.
Choking's all, between.

Little black smell,
what do you tell?
Go back under
your ledge, smelly troll.

Sorry. Moi so utter.
Gutterly and down.
Cheek leak side way ground
to ground.

Upon, upon. A dizzy rub me in.
Terror blacksmell dream that no let
ter. Here shall ev. Ermoi.
Sh nev. er. no.n.thing. no mean...

But bookish boy he's back! Sees moi and heeves
this sideways volume out and oap and *whoah*!
He offers up his veryown card and
stack/blip/blink/stamp/flop/stack/back/it's/

littlewhile all
his. Pour moi!

HYDRANGEA

Peel the petals back, the spillage back,
the fists of paleness back from smouldering blue

to the color of fire to the color of fire burnt to time.
Now, by holding the stem and backing a long way off,

all the way out of your life to a ledge
above a dry pool, you could own the flower.

But the Other has set out a vase.
So now it is a charcoal sketch

of how rain wishes, crookedly, to fall.
Tenderness in the junctures.

Stemming from a pool into which the skater vanishes.
As into the lion's eye tameness.

As into the body with your voice inside it,
water-in-a-vase,

and into the body with O's voice inside it,
water-in-a-vase,

finally goes the flower.
The single blackened eyestalk.

What seeing did.
What desire wants to be shriven to the shape of.

Why in the world
this flower.

The Yellow House Alone in Snow

The house looked out
for itself
through twin windows

and saw trees ticking. Pelts
pelting. A dense considering
considering it.

What could the house pull
the shutters shut with,
curtains?

What could the world warm its vast
countenance with,
space?

So, nothing was displaced;
not house, not world, not the sense
of wanting to be other than like this.

The moon has an other side
that soaks up the world's radios
if the world radios. The world knows this.

And the boy, shouting, has an other side
he puts his fist through to, but,
the house assures him, his room is still his room.

This otherness, though, stayed.
Like snowflakes falling in the shape,
in the silence and the velvet, of dead moths,

it made the house stand still
as though all migrations
—glaciers, peoples, atoms—

had come to their ends in it,
might be all there was to it,
history, pre- and post-, rising up

along the clapboards as
snow kept falling and therefore rising up,
encasing the house like concrete slowly

poured into the cast of a monument
that had, invisibly, always, cocooned
the house and some substantial portion of the world.

For what was the yellow house still standing?
For which idea?
For whom?

Inside, the tepid air stood still, a done-in lung,
and the house sank into the jaundiced sleep of
something born so young and so deprived of so

much warmth it needs to drink the sun.
And it would be sleeping still,
guzzling, nuzzling, gargling, snarling *yellow, yellow*,

were it not for the sharpened tear
of the boy's imperial red sled
approaching, approaching, the boy

returning from far beyond the world,
as, in the dream of the beginning and the end,
the pony returns, ice-shod, head bowed,

glittering with tiny bells that stay tiny
as he approaches, almost grown up now,
pulling at the rope to drag

two knives through snow,
excising a swath in his wake as long
as the path through a life to the planet

of infinite and undisturbed forgiveness
of nothing toward nothing
in the face of yellow, spectral nothing

which is the land and landscape
and the cape Something wears, flourishing,
turning Its back upon us with a flourish

in the snorting eye of red, the laughing eye of yellow,
for warmth and further flourishing, and for
us to walk upon, to dance across the gutter upon,

because we are regal, and the house, from which
the seeing comes which is also the thing which sees,
the *does* which is the *is*, is yellow, and is flourishing.

GLOVE

The story of the life of hesitation.
    Or.
The story of the life of crash and burn.

The body in which the life is sheathed
    in either story
is like a bedtime glove

put on to aid
    the absorption of unguents
but found in shreds at daybreak

as if it had been peeled from the windshield
    of a yellow car, a bandage
furred by frost, or milk.

I don't know which destiny,
    the one of frost or milk,
takes the most desiring or the longest path to come to.

The universe of milk fills us with velvet
    knowing that the universe of frost
occludes our ever having known.

But *something* wrings its hands,
    and we cover up, or comfort,
that thing with our own hands--

Either way we feel
    the story make a fist
just before what's done

is finally done.

II.

THE YELLOW HOUSE GIVES TOUR
NUMBER ONE OF THE BIG ART BOOK

O.K. Kandinsky arranges the neurons into temporarily breathing humhums. The glint is right now being so that the eyebrow of earth sharp dance with pretty chasm that ski. If you try to exit before the ski is done, the house-thing in there houses your eye awhile while a eye your houses there in thing-house the exit to try to if. Kandinsky sure CanDoSky. Belly why yes he can. O.K. Keep it hanging. Now here is hisstory.

Once he had a horse too like I do and everybody got on it and they all turned blue. Then there were just four of them and nobody was riding only blue and wanting money. So since the horse was free to go he came on over here and as you'll see sometime soon he has been doing a little painting of his own. Which the woman doesn't like. A primitive says she. But she should know about outsider now being pretty funky her self some her—well. Well, anyway, today we CanDoSky. Tomorrow we might be where we cannot do sky and so today were is here and loving Candosky. We are allowing our wholentire rouged smear thing coming out of our heart to dosky. You think it matters if it has a heart? What heart *is* is candosky. First you get rid extra else in some other paintings then you can just dosky. Me I have some stairs above the attic. Candosky friend Clay he put some ladders and some climbing up blocks in his. But you don't have to have. See, you can justdosky. Heart is the whole colorshape of Can. Universe is Do. Sky, you pick your own. Now, O.K., you can turn other lights.

Remember old distance man we saw dying in his brain first? Well, he died. Doing almost all sky all the time deep in there toward the end. And old woman who kept loving him was doing least halfsky. But now must say it is her belly turn soon so soon so I and some other big book will be back.

In Dreams She is Permitted
to Return to the Floating Room

Sometimes her life attends her
                    riding up in the glass box
but air's pinched   chairs few
                    a hair hook reels her back up

                        the room says there there
            hand making a face   out of coins and tears

        hips still make one hip   *there*
                                            there

                        the air is a still
                            ravaged   still
secret-heavy like   the plans of earth

                                        outside   's forge

and forgery
                            ugliness in the machines

        O hoist
            her again   gin

sweating
        of clear grain

ONE DEER AND ONE DEER DECOY
IN A SLANT OF LIGHT

What if love should call you
          to a thing not of this world?
And not of spirit, either,
          or spirits, or ether,

but fiberglass and paint and
          a marble from your childhood
schoolyard for an eye?
          And what if your

sweet jaggedness
          turns out to be this path
along which your private
          palenesses have flashed?

Gorged breath, gorged haunch
          misfire—you've
flinderated echelons of green.
          And someone, *god*, has *seen*.

Too late to try your muzzle
          upon that shining muzzle,
and match your eye to that milk eye
          and sidle your ache-shape up—

The woods is dull nickels, dark pockets.
          The clearing is what you gave.
Now there is only the yellowed horn
          twisting apart desire from its grave.

Shh every. Shhh ok. Here! Tada! Show!

No? Another no? Oh no.

The horse is kind of shy about his *Boyhorse* picture. Yes no yes no no yes *no*. Will not let us see. Says that, if else sees, he will not ever *be* again.

But lovie horse, I said. Say moi!

Not even moi.

Ah-it's-a-horse-poof-gone. Is what he thinks. He really thinks.

So I must cancel no wing. Of early horsewerks. Forget you hear. Uh huh. There's no to-die-for-fetlock, no infinite nose slope, and no how boy goes down. No which wind is mane which tooth which hair. Forget. Is not. Just isn't. Never. No. Just don't.

BELOW THE CELLAR OF THE YELLOW HOUSE
THERE IS ANOTHER SET OF STAIRS

You are not a drill or a mole or at a film.
Not that meteor destined for earth's tomb.
Your thighs bear no message from the yellow pollen surface.
Hell is somewhere else and you've already been to the womb.

You will need these stairs.

You are not blind cave-fish, not deep,
translucent crab, not scuttle, not squirm.
Not time enough in your life to adapt.
And you are not just mind, not just a bunch of words.

You will need these stairs.

So here's your coat of sprightly arms,
and here's your staff, a little worn.
And you will need this mantle, as earth needs its mantle
to cool itself as inner and outer are re-formed.

And you will need these stairs.

You can have this mask, this set
of masks, soft on the face-side.
And here is a bun in the shape of a storm,
according to your hunger and your sighs.

You will need these stairs.

Did we mention how the landings are ivory
as horse's teeth if you get down that far?
How, willingly, not wavering,
with his long velvet jaw ajar...

So you must take these stairs,

jagged as your heart. Because the Other vanished.
Because it is the nature of sweet hovering to elapse.
And stay in you, small wind, rough pearl. The silver sound
of blood-borne stars, collapsed.

You will need these stairs.

The Boy Asks

house why don't you have

a slide from my window.

that goes into a pool.

that stays still all the time.

so the baby turtles could come.

and totally dark windows at night.

so they don't think you're the moon and go in you.

and die.

and ghost crabs.

and more of that gold hay.

and a chocolate horse this Easter.

he made me write that.

if it wouldn't freak him out.

I wrote that.

world peace robot carrots my dad.

healthy carrot-flavored robots for him hah.

and a castle.

no offense.

Yellow House Isogloss

Across

1. Valve in a horse's heart
the same shape as the horse
2. Flower taxidermy
3. In reverse order, said of floors
4. Aureole; fog life vest
5. Color between receiving and opening
6. 14th c. palace inhabited only by horses
7. Seventh ingredient of contentment
8. Deepest place in the body
9. To fashion entirely of mullions
10. Likely bridle color on colorless horse
11. What world
12. Happy-in-the-grid; plunge
13. Special thread; also said of a shaft
14. Found at the end of the stairs
15. Name of the boy
15. Other name of the boy

Down

1. Strongest threshold
2. Kind of stoop
3. To be blinded by scent of yellow smoke
4. Coll. for bitter straw
5. Love's photographic side (archaic)
6. Desultory, as of a room without birds
7. Shard, usually red
8. Reconciled; crocodiled
9. The number of allowances needed
9. The number of straws in the world
10. Hay (greeting)
11. Chocolate (v.)
12. Soul at its known apex
13. Meal consisting entirely of yellow food
14. Urgent unguent
15. Other Other

THE HUNT

Rain lately, tropic.
Light, myopic.
Mood, mythic.

Shine thoughts, stichic.
Longing, for a picnic.
Three petals, the topic.

Talk in town of trillium.
Talk of a walk to find it.
Endangered! Exotic! Grown-up delirium.

The boy wants to go.
To blend in so deep
among the throng of villagers

his own desire which involves a certain
shovel and spade
disappears into mist and midst.

And would it not be a good thing to bring beauty home?
Re-root it in privacy? Re-root in it a privacy?
Make of it an altar and invite the man

who seems, now, to suffer
from lack of something three-petaled
to bow down to, body, mind, and soul,

who moves, since he moved out,
around the thing that hides in him,
ghost-dance, lost-chance, a gulp

between him and the boy?
But out there are these tripods sturdy as green promising.
Out there, if you lie upon your back as in a shallow grave

and focus three inches above your earthen face is
a flower darker red than women's darkest blood,
whose velvet tripartite bell seeing robs, and rings . . .

Why else has the boy been walking
slow as geologic time,
head bent to ground?

House, can't he go?
Forest, can't you spare one?
Do-gooders, can't you look the other way?

Soil, loosen.
Forest, listen in.
Yellow, daven, dapple.

Big guy, little big guy,
give it up.
Give in.

THE PROPHET CASTS A SPELL
FOR RELEASING THE OTHER BACK INTO THE YELLOW AIR

Those packages of harm you have been keeping in the separate warehouse?
Your life of the single fork and sharpened spoon?

The five oranges' skin gone loose on their slick bodies?
The skeleton smile? Fashion? That tune?

The field you would burn with everyone in it?
The smoke still on your tongue?

You may bring all your sweet things
though they'll count for nothing now that we've begun.

The weather today is red.
What else could we expect?

That a new idea of form
would align the blood?

To be stapled to green heaven?
That kindness was enough?

That stones brought from the Parthenon
would guide you to a bluff

and a dive blue enough
to wash away your fear?

Depth is all there is.
Astonishment

passing like a huge fish
though no words bubble out.

And straws of light. Nothing
to drink but straws of light.

You have my permission to weep
seven blue tears

before these depths
are sealed.

Well back come! Hah! Well, today, we, are, doing,
OneSadFace. Made of Klee. When you don't lift the pencil that is what
you get this guy is OneSadFace. Even if he had not lifted for eye/eye/
moth, it still would be the same, said, sad, still, kley.

Is how. Something er is er *in* their you juster know so you
make grid and when the klay is dry you sift it through the grid. And
whoah! Three hooks, one longloop line, but nopole noarm no, so
OneSadFace. Next time fishing you should try to fish for something.
Me, I'm thinking *horsey* so I make horsehook horseshape and whoah!

But Klee reely need idee. So bad. So he sees thees idee see:

Grid Grid Grid What What What
Grid Grid Grid Grid Grid Grid
Crid Gild Gild Grid Grid Grid
Grab Grid Grid Grab Grid Grid
Grid Ridd Grid OhCraprahbdid

(oh thank you thank you oh it was nothing no was it)

It is very happy inthegrid when you don't cook for something.
"not sea not sea not sea" see? Happy-in-the-grid. Me I am full grid.
Updown rightleft house-stuffed. Mantle lintel mullion ocean up down
up down happy-in-the-grid. Shingle, shinglehair, squarehair, ah!
Happy in the grid. Even when OneSadFace, even when LostAllWay,
you have you can have your happy-in-the-grid.

What?

You think we should not show old dying belly distance woman
this OneSadFace? You think it's HisFace? HerFace? You think you
happy picture need for happy-in-the-grid?

WHAT THE WHOLE HORSE DOES

It started when he rode out
of a sound he didn't, himself, hear,
the boy already on his back
already completely old,
the animal already in him.

That was that.

And the woman who felt his hooves
to be the whole of love.
And the memory of hooves
like the ground tearing inside her.

That is still that.

Now the whole horse burns
cold blue in the yellow grass.
Not seeing any other horses.

That.

Thought is Allowed

Thought is allowed.
Mink in its own skin.
Bothering no one.
Not letting outside in.

Thought is allowed.
Deep into the hill.
As for the hillside,
sunny, still.

Thought is allowed.
Never mind what kind
of furious petals
pave the mind.

Thought is allowed.
Now. Never. Mind
cannot bear it.
Mind, its own kin.

Thought is allowed.
Lace shreds like death.
Not yours. Ours.
In it, our breaths.

Thought is allowed.
It yields to itself.
World that confounds it?
--Mute globe on a shelf.

Thought is allowed.
Here is a letter.
Inside, a treatise
on the uses of glitter.

Thought is allowed.
Once is wise.
Hold me. Now.
But now is twice.

Thought is allowed
though it sicken the thinker.
Unto... Old... Too...
(See?) Thicker... thicker...

Thought is allowed
its own meadow.
All-leaf bouquet,
bitter, better.

Thought is allowed.
More unto the end!
Thought is allowed,
and the house it tends.

HORSE BETWEEN TOURS

Well the horse he has stopped making anymore pictures.
Where, I want to say, is your medium your stretch? He looks a way.
You don't want in glint gridsky? He looks a way. Did boy fall off your
eye? He looks a way. Well come you any way next tour? He looks a
way. Get yr own inspire card to check out full books of horse? Horse,
he looks a way. You modeling me some goodside? He looks. He looks a
way.

Now what did we do we doctor we?

Dabbed a little yellow on his tailbrush.

CONTAINED

After you have swum to the inland island

after you have toweled off with the giant leaf

and rolled in the black resin garment

and scaled the hill like a forgotten saint

and gained the pointed dwelling

after the bellrope brushes your face

one knot for every hesitation of your life

that ends that will end in a burnished bell

once you step back into the footprints

once your arms make a roof above your thoughts

once you are dangling from the rusted crucible

of every furious dissemblance you hath done

and the lake gathers round and glistens with the sound

that carries that turns that licks

the barren and forfeits all clamber and slays

the surfeit of the sun and winds time

to a tether and hooks it on your heart

what then, what then, will you have done?

And how and what should you presume? Exhume?

The coin hewn in half? And if you picked it up,

and began right there on the earthen floor

to scratch out your chance, your yin of a green

and, deeper, your gold, interminable dream?

And tyranny of riches kept

that flattens your thought to a mold?

Now bring on the keepers and the truck.

The packages, the alms.

Cough up your little night

and render your drop

now all the snug particulars are gone.

III.

LIGHTS OVER THE SEA

Matches in the distance, little wet troops,
strike until you're bare, until the nothing that you are
rises up against a raveling

for tonight will be a rending or a plume.
The heart staggering against a frame
where the child leans, milk-and-honey mouthed.

*****

she came to a place. sala.
where she had been before. sala.

in the other the beautiful life. sala.
where she'd been allowed to be. sala.

the hard and the possible soft. sala.
ache that recognized ache. sala.

so it is. sala. again. sala.
the yellowing blueprint re-conceived. sala.

*****

She walked to the side of herself
where she had trained the horse to walk

what friends there were admired
the floating rhinestone bridle

trotting now, now cantering,
now bobbing like a little boat's

glinty fringe of lights way out
upon a tossing sea

and so it came to her how through
that stuttered instant

four   feet float   she
might slip through

*****

And then her eyesight waned
there being nothing quite yet to look at

and for a while she couldn't eat
but no one said my how

fashionable your skeleton
rising like a hanger through the yellow dress of flesh

but still her hair kept growing
what the child had rendered nickel

she transmuted to a hue somewhere
between august and locust

and twirled into horns and cathedrals
and waves and cries and burnishings

and a final flouishing comma curling
duty off for good from

the like-a-cormorant-lifting-sense
she had again of beauty

and then she stormed the house
her decision ablaze

* * * * *

Late, in some kind of day or other.

Standing at the field's edge
in tall black pants and chiselled heels.

Late in the day. Late in her life.
Tardy. Quarry. Tarnishings and turns.

There, by the tall grasses slated for a burn,
the villagers approaching with torches and shovels.

A swarm of promises. Seep and weep.
The day undoing certain actions done to it.

Little Day, Tendril, extending to some shore.

* * * * *

It isn't known, still,
how, or how it was, that she
began to pack, first the
easy things, hats and scarves out
of season, then some uncracked
books then the boy's first

derelict drawings whose
red and yellow torsos still
untwirled from a DNA of mist

then the cookbook whose one output the man
had disdained and she had loved and then the extra
curtain-weight, a coin in her palm, something
about billowing or being unable to billow, then
old distance woman's letters
to the babyfaced doomed pilot, and then,

when the house had gone into a wildness like a clearing
to which the animals are suddenly afraid to come,
an opening overrun by drills, plinths, hammers, mowers,
plasterers, arrangers, scripts, truths, sudden aisles

she stole—it was midnight—having surrendered all
but one key, she stole back in for the lights, the necklace
of little white lights on the dogwood, she took back her attempt
to make something beautiful out of the former scene

*****

And she said to the boy: *Come.*
And he said to the horse: *Come.*
And the horse said to the house: *You sweet old towering tottering oldie,*
                                  of horse, of house, of course.

Above the Attic of the Yellow House
There is Another Set of Stairs

You'll know by the yellowing lowering,
and by the sheen of boxes bathed

in a broken, aureate glow, and by the weight
as of a league of ochre-throated feathers,

and by the silent spiralings
of tubes plugged at both ends,

and by the snarlings of wire
debrided to the copper veins of the objects

you've despaired of, saved for and despaired of,
and by the single stalk and frosted bulb

about to flower downward toward
the tiny human meadow where you stand.

You can climb here any time you want.
You can sway among these ruins and runes.

Like a bee in amber, something of you stays
and the hum of you keeps climbing.

Lyric Interlude

Everything a flower or a shout or sleep.
Time glistening and skidding.
Reasons glistening and skidding.

A gull's cry or the boy's or hers.

All that seeking after.
All that seeking, after.
The hurt in the distance grinds on,

shells on a beach, sharp shells.

But she opens the ornate door to the meadow
not to the story of the meadow.
Flowerbox sans box.

She isn't afraid of beauty and in fact wears beautiful things

by which the meadow knows when
she has passed that she has passed,
a woman in the middle of a life,

pebble in the middle of a sea.

It is not the case that every one of us
is a princess and every time we move an arm
the great climatic shifts, coming floods and so forth.

On this yellow planet the little umbrellas in the drinks just suddenly
are there.

Yellow Pilgrimage

Here is the prophet
coming down out of the hills

in relentless rain,
his prints dissolving instantly to earth.

Slowly he descends, and disappears behind a ridge,
and surfaces, and goes on recommencing,

stitching an old question to the ground,
his robe a little flag or blurred flourish,

a pen, or errant ink,
white, wet, on a dim page.

And here is the roof
nailed down of course by rain

where he comes at last to argue the woman's case
in front of the suntanned gods.

Rivers appear, and dry, and crack,
and appear and wash the animals into them

and dry, and crack, and the bleached furs are how
he describes her want.

He has a little jar for the wet tears.
He has a little notebook for the dry.

She has for him some stems
from the place where the ash

of those who meet
when they are already graying

makes the greens
so green.

TO ARRIVE AT YOUR DOOR

To arrive in black velvet for breakfast.

To appear one thread at a time
like a breeze across the galaxies.

Warp of my autumn hair. Weft of your dear autumn hair.

To transmit a package wrapped in fur
warm as the original animal inside.

To ring to keep on ringing.

The story we will write of us.
The things they will say of us.

To story to thing to say to say *now*.

To assume the dearest position.
To kiss contrition's tip.

To say to the rain you were wrong.

To go forward to the beginning.
To arrive at the edge still stinging.

To ring to keep on ringing.

To put lips to the axis
shining red in old-planet light.

To say to the companionable abyss

we will crush particular persimmons.
We will grind deepest light.

We will ravish every previous goodnight

to arrive at last at this door
bringing want, itself, to shore.

WAVES

Some days now the house is like a houseboat
and she will wave from the floating door
and the dear one waves from the floating letter

    bobbing like a paper hat upon the waves,

and an incense or innocence will rise like smoke
from the waters although you cannot see it,
not even when the boy cuts through it

    in his little dinghy on the way to school,

ringing his bell as if he were an ordinary boy,
the carpenter's ruler coiled
in his pocket like a yellow snake

    for show-and-tell.

But now, while the boy is away,
and the house is obscured among drifting
angles and aims and aches and wants

    for nothing, softly knocking

against the small ladder off the dock
where it is moored to silence,
and the question of stairs-to-stars

    is infinite and infinitely far away

and death and love are not, for once,
the only hosts of silence and solace,
and space itself, color itself, motion itself

    is holy, holy,

and what's outside the body is time
and what's inside the body is time
and just now, they meet upon waves

which wave and wave to time...

Hours like this
belong to the house
and we are wrong to take them.

But, released from the winter of our life,

let us fold a boat out of our old desires
and launch it out upon the surface
of what, shimmering,

is.

Saffron cube comets lick,
orbiting the binary system
Heart-and-Mind.

Door knocker glinting
like a little dead star's
cheeky Eagle Scout grin.

If the man comes through and sends
the telescope for Christmas
how can the woman level

and explain the farthest things
to the boy? The floor having drifted out
from under them so gradually.

The way years went.
Face first into the basin of stars.
A gesture. A something. Consent.

Old Distance Woman Has Asked
the Yellow House for a Book

Ah! Special request! Well. We don't know how to read AnyMysterious well really AnyAny made of LittleBlackSmell, but she really likes Mysterious, especially Mysterious where WhoDone figure out It plus extra HerbHawkThing.

So trying. So, we're trying. We want to find a good one, one of the last good ones for old distance belly woman. All she can swallow now is a GoodBlackSmell.

The real mysterious is how is this new story going to *get* to her...hmm...from our mysterious yellow voice in the distance. Hmm. That's a mysterious. Whoah! That's what she wants! Hah! We already story!

Ahem. *One there was a yellow voice, and one there was a be-a-u-tiful woman.* (She like that, and she *like* that!) *Well. She heard the beautiful yellow voice* (moi) *come out of nowhere. Ah, says she, I think I will go into the No now to find the Beautiful.*

Well how do you like that mysterious? That wholestory there! LifeDeathYell in there! But her bellygoing pretty slow, so O.K. we say some more, some slow more for her.

What?

You want to say some more? You want me to?

We both.

Let see... She had a beautiful Other war kilt so that that. Different kind of BotherOther that. That just that.

Let see. She had the woman well baby of course then years nice years. Then her man go off to mysty war in mister brain. Letters home then not. So she start painting paint. Of flowers staying still.

All very mysterious how flowers flowr still-ly and beaut. Now her little nurseroom fullup sipcup of staystill fleur. On the walls and inher innerds the too growing kind. Rampant my-sterio-yes in there. Part of her hurrying toward yellow. Part of her dragging her yellow foot. More and more myster flower...

But ahem she call for more Mysterious to read! Quick that we can do. All so myster now and she asking more mysterious! Wow she some kind of old distance woman! Where we were were we well.

yellow yellow yellow
beautiful beautiful woman
yellow yellow yellow
beautiful beautiful woman

She things the mysterious is where the voice comes from. But yellow is mysterious and she is mysterious and yellow belly flowers are more and more mysterious. So. Maybe if she try going back and forth and back.

yellow yellow yellow   belly belly belly
             hah! sapsucker! hah!
myster myster myster   pain pain pain
             hah! it rhyme with GoodMan name!

It is like the horse swishing fly, a little yellow on his tail. Forth back forth. Paint her own beautiful mysterious. She a whole story of that.

Sorry having trouble thinging the mysteriouses she asks. Last good stories need lots of just the right mysterious. Best we can do today. The boy he wrote it down for me and off it sent went.

But now we need a story for the boy, he so already bellymiss her.
Horse one I think.

LIKE A HORSE

First death was coming like a horse
        walking
and then death was coming like a horse
        running
and then old distance woman put on
        the velvet visage brown
breath apple teeth so as not to
        be thrown

This happened where the sun struck dune
        upon dune
this happened in a way that no one could
        assume the
two sails bobbing on the distant thirst were
        not there
to rescue her before the rest of the head rose
        and reared

We tried to pet her we knew better than to ride her
        we threw
carrot-colored books on the extinction
        of horses
and gleaming books by inquisitionists
        of horses
and slim books about how utterly untrustworthy some
        horses are but

they kept they kept on coming she got
        so she
could speak a little horse   sweating in the latitudes
        the nettle
and the gentian she   mint and leech   trade and weed
        flesh back hair
sense and whip   she shoe and crab   she radish chestnut
mackeral bean
        she balm   balm   she fly

Dear One

Your lifetime moving through the darkness like a train,
the single lamp like a match on a long stem
lighting, always, the next moment but not this one.

A huge hand hurls the ties just in time.
A friend's soggy death, ancestral blues-strewn plea,
abandonings and ravishments, trapdoor that will not stitch—
crossings, metal on metal, cues, smoke.

I see you. From somewhere in that darkness. I see you.

To either side the darkness
like a tongue across the plain.
It levels mountains and crosses
the democracies of tuft and asphalt it asks
for money it holds
its breath for fear of saying your name

and eats through the
five or six nodules of wealth
that govern every shoelace and the
fate of ice on earth,

and goes to Washington
and prys open with its teeth the
inner and the inner-inner chambers of power
and blows the darkness
back up into their faces and opens

its dark lips and calls home all things
made of metal and stupidity
and any human kindness
wrongfully deployed
and smooths and licks clean the cries
that flare in the distance

and still your lifetime
has been moving in the darkness and my
lifetime has been moving in the darkness and we
are both alive in this chapter of the earth

in which you kiss me
on one and then all of my
four corners, first the right instep, the steps' shallow
grave, and then the left instep where is inscribed
the names who had abandoned me and those
I have abandoned, and then
the right palm where the girl rubbed her
two pennies for the milk
the government paid for the rest of
into a hot mitten song
and then the left palm that stuttered round
the ashes of her first beloved who chose
to walk the plank of this chapter of the earth—

you open that fist again unto a distance
and bring my four corners together like a bow—

come seal me in the darkness
of this shameful century
haggard in its youth,
cover my mouth
completely with your mouth,
summon me, startle me
to sweetness, to our task.

RED AND BLACK DAYS

Sometimes now they gather at the table,
the woman and the boy and the dear one
whose cheer has come to stay
along with the royal possibilities

a day of checkers affords.
Crown me! the boy will say.
Kings and kings and kings.
The boy moves them forward

and back in space and time,
and sideways, and snake-like, and
like hopscotch and gazelles.
A little red fiefdom of his own design

with a side street for the underlings
to dwell in. The pauper population
growing, cheering! Tossing up
their thin black caps!

A Pattern Language

Let there be a house, two windows, a chair.

Let there be a small house
with two open windows and a chair
so there can be the lilac from the left, the sumac from the right.

And let it be made of a wood the old and the young agree on,
with a chair the young can climb in and the old can get up out of
between windows out of which each sees what each can see.

Or make it where meadow meets mew,
with two small windows high enough
and all her old summers blowing through.

Or is it, if it's for her, a dwelling underhill,
a chair where love sits down, and slits
where thought shines, still.

Or just an invisible house
and a hard, invisible chair.
Invisible curtains to hide in. For she remembers that air:

a room boiled down from light,
a little table, and a chair,
to the story written there:

a house made out of sound
with all the chairs in a row,
and when the music stops it is herself, excused,

and the pattern holds.
No need then for the windows.
No need for the chairs.

Just one house made of earth,
with a chair for the boy to sing in
when he is alone without them,

one window on the east his mother,
one window on the west his men, and a door,
for when the ripeness comes, to ride out of, and back again.

For it's one gong for the mother,
and one gong for the men,
and a bell on the harness of the earth

: all. And back again.

Once upon time, the horse took old distance woman on a very long trip. So long that she finally said would it be o.k. if I fall asleep against your neck horse and horse said what oh uh I must have been walking in my sleep. So they went on like that for a while. Into the soft sleeping distance.

After a while of riding through a clearness clear as the water in the tank before the first fish goes in, the horse and the old woman came to a place where there was a circle of light. The old woman yawned and stretched out her two legs—she looked like an upside down scarecrow—to make the light just the right size. And the horse sighed and stretched out his four legs—and of course then down they went! And then they had a nice better sleep. And then they woke up hungry. And so they ate some light.

What?

Oh, when you eat light it fills back up right away.

The horse stayed with the old woman quite a while. Eating the clear. Drinking the clear. Trotting around the clear. It was very easy on the hooves. Bales and bales of clear. Clear dreams. Clear jokes. Clear apples, clear beer, clear deer. Then the old woman said I think you should go back to the boy. And the horse said I think *you* should go back to the boy. So they thought about that for a while.

Then the old woman who was always good at planning trips with crisp accurate picnics said listen horse I think the clearness might be a horse-crossing-only kind of clearness. So they thought about that for a while.

Then the horse said well ok but while I'm gone will you start making us a nice clear house which of course she had already started doing.

And so the horse went back. For the boy.

Pursuit of the Yellow House

The way the body builds a house
        around a grain in its own sight,
objecting to the object, mulling

      and mouthing it, washing and rubbing it,
        making a little gem of pain
the body soothes and swaddles in a small red

      pearl it sets upon the outer grasslands
        of the eye—
did the house arise around you

      because of *something*, the barren
        possible, a tender, trembling mux
that flowed from you and cooled?

      Or did it first appear
        in the distance—
note-on-a-staff, hand-shaped bird,

      flickerings' ledger, cornice-of-a-cure—
        so that you,
Manger-Monger, Dank-

      Hankerer, Daffodil-Whisperer, Termite-
        Diviner and Would-Be Curator
of the Secret Stair where you did and you

      did and you wept and you
        lay down and
no more than usual did the sun refuse you,

pursued—
           with wood with wooing with words—
this casket of sun this what-you-hath-done this

           deckled abyss this claw-colored *is*.
                   Mute vial.
Tear-on-a-string

           the color of use.
                   Amber ampul
to contain our   —all.

           To set us loose.

S P U Y T E N D U Y V I L
Meeting Eyes Bindery
Triton